Kay Eck

Divorce:
a love story

A surprising tale of the power of
self-love to heal every last thing

@iamselfpub
www.iamselfpublishing.com

For
Andrew, Weston, Evan & Audrey
with everlasting gratitude to Fred, and

The Wayshowers:
Wanda Vitale, Theresa Luttenegger & Kaia Ra

The Heartholders:
Chris Denz, Alexa Schill, Jan Courter, Diana Schieke, Sandy
Dixon, Meggan Riley, Nancy Petrone, Mary Lou Quirk,
Laurie Alfano & Frank Alfano

The Lightkeepers:
Donna Miceli, Elizabeth Gresher, Gretchen Eck, Amy
Merritt, Sheri Bagwell, Michelle Benson, Jon Benson, Sarah
Lindgren, Christy Guyer, Mary Clare McNulty, Lisa Bodett,
Autumn Spravka, Martina Segovia, Nancy Eck, Shirley Eck,
Kim Trager, CJ Hathaway, Bridget Hay, Maureen Rooney,
Tera Abelson, and

My beloved Shine Family,

The Diamonds,

The Sophia Code Tribe, and

The I AM Self Publishing Team.

My eyes so fix

upon your image

that whatever I gaze at

I imagine you.

Fakhruddin Iraqi, "My eyes so fix",
trans. William Chittick and Peter Lamborn Wilson

Introduction

This is what shocked me most: After nearly 30 years of marriage to a man I truly loved, guiding four fantastic children into adulthood, creating a slew of wonderful memories in several welcoming homes, I was so ashamed to be getting a divorce that, for months, I didn't tell anyone other than a few close friends. Many months. There are people who might consider themselves to be my friends (and family) who were never told. By me anyway.

What's shocking about this? Fred and I weren't perfect, we made mistakes along the way, but neither of us had done anything wrong. There was absolutely nothing to be ashamed of.

After years of suspecting our relationship was no longer serving us, very long periods of hoping that it was just a phase and diligent efforts in counseling, in the early summer of 2017, we began the process of uncoupling. It was not long before I was drowning in a torrent of emotion. In addition to the incredible sadness we both felt at parting ways after so many good years together and, of course, disappointing the children whom we love so much, I was contending with a dark cloud of shame. And I couldn't understand why.

I began rising at dawn to meditate and to feel the peace of the space between days. On one of those days, without forethought, I began to write. I wrote every morning for a long while before realizing that what was pouring forth was a very real and raw story of the consequences of open-hearted vulnerability. I had earlier vowed to face every heartbreaking day with as much honesty as I could – owning what was mine, digging deeply for the underlying issues and showering everything and everyone with as much love as I could muster. I just wanted my family to continue to be about love, not loss.

The honesty nearly wrecked me. The writing saved me.

It allowed me to process everything I was experiencing. And when the writing felt done, it had become a tale of awakening, self-discovery, healing and transformation. Though mutual and amicable, a still-painful divorce is what catapulted me onto a path of deep reconciliation with myself. It forced me, or more precisely, allowed me, to cast a sometimes harsh light onto every shadowy thing I believed about myself. What I eventually revealed was a soul so beautiful, an essence so bright, it brought me to tears – regularly!

And that is why my story, rooted in pain and sorrow, is a love story, bursting with triumph.

* * *

I remember the public scorn for the actress Gwyneth Paltrow when her publicist released a statement in 2014 announcing that she and her husband, Chris Martin, were working through a "conscious uncoupling" which everyone understood, of course, to be a divorce.

The concept was so unfamiliar that it was either quickly dismissed or roundly derided. That a husband and wife could part ways as lovingly as they had come together just didn't seem plausible. Especially in Hollywood.

We find ourselves in an age when we are marrying in our 20s and 30s and dying in our 80s and 90s. It is an era of rapid awakening in which growth is the hallmark of personal development. How likely is it that each person in a marriage will evolve in the same way, at the same rate, over the course of 20, 40, or even 60 years? Is it not possible for two clear-headed people to decide that their partnership has reached its fulfillment and amicably conclude it?

I now know how much courage is required to do this difficult work. It wasn't until I began my own journey through divorce that I understood how entrenched we are in the unexamined story of it. Like countless others, I had unconsciously accepted what my cultural upbringing had taught me about divorce – that it is a hate-fueled process marked by rancorous in-fighting that traumatizes everyone involved. I began to suspect that a large portion of the resulting pain derives from our mindless buy-in of that version of the divorce story. And then I began to wonder what would happen if I wrote a new version for myself and my family. This is the crux of consciousness – to question everything and to choose for yourself. Spoiler Alert: Being conscious through the divorce process does not make it easier. There will be grappling with difficult emotions, uncovering uncomfortable truths and choosing peace and love over position and power. Again and again and again.

Conscious Uncoupling required me to consider these questions:

What is the way to best honor the relationship I entered into in love, the relationship that created the children I cherish, the bond that not only sustained me for many years but also created the classroom in which I learned the most?

How do I uphold the beautiful, messy, imperfect humanness of my one-time partner in life?

How do I tackle an impossibly difficult task with integrity?

How do I find a way to nurture my own broken heart without trampling on the heart of another?

How do I add sweetness where there may be bitter disappointment?

How do I create a future for myself and my family that continues to be grounded in love?

* * *

I know there are divorce scenarios far more challenging than mine. I know there are relationships in which the consciousness may be completely one-sided.

Ending a marriage can be a gut-wrenching course through which one attempts to re-craft a loving and respectful relationship with his or her more or less willing partner. If my husband and I hadn't both strongly committed to a positive outcome, I'm not sure how we would have fared.

As it was, I was stepping on landmines of my own heart. The going got pretty rough. Deep and ancient wounds were unearthed, and I had to constantly remind myself to tread gently, breathe deeply and rest often. I had to reaffirm my conviction that my higher self, the sacred essence that is me, had arranged for me to have these experiences with these people so that I could see more clearly the truth of who I really am. Who we all are.

Ultimately, the work doesn't have to be mutual because the self-discovery that heals is, necessarily, a solitary route. But there is so much fruit to bear, even when we are out in the field alone.

One of the gifts of my divorce is that while my family remains a complicated drama with a big cast of evolving characters, when I look in the mirror now, I see a version of myself that is truer than the pre-divorce incarnation.

I have been rewritten by my own love.

My sincerest wish is that, here, you find comfort, courage and support on your own journey and that you can receive your challenges as gifts. My hope is that you allow yourself to be rewritten too as you learn the truth of who you really are.

With all my love,
Kay Eck

a billion stars go spinning through the night,

blazing high above your head.

But in you is the presence that

will be, when all the stars are dead.

Rainer Maria Rilke, "Buddha in Glory",
trans. Stephen Mitchell

Part One

The Hours slid fast – as Hours will,

Clutched tight, by greedy hands –

So faces on two Decks, look back,

Bound to opposing lands –

Emily Dickinson, "There came a Day at Summer's full"

1.

My husband of nearly thirty years wakes me at 6 am to ask if we can talk before he leaves for work. At first I think I am dreaming.

I rise from a sleep-deprived trance and drag myself downstairs to his office and my familiar perch opposite his desk. The windows are still shut against an unusually cool May morning. He sits across from me and with tears in his eyes, tells me he is concerned about our relationship.

By this time, lawyers have been interviewed, a settlement has been drafted and we are fully engaged in the heart-wrenching process of becoming no-longer-a-couple.

I am not so muddled that I miss the irony of this scene and, in fact, how infrequent these discussions have been. I cannot help but wonder if all the difficulty we now face could have been avoided had either of us been able to have these discussions over the years.

He reminds me of our pledge to avoid the spiral of bitterness that often swallows couples in the throes of divorce. I remind myself that divorce is not something I want to go through alone.

I don't know yet if conscious uncoupling is the right terminology for what we are doing. I am conscious of pausing now to choose how I want things to go between us as a new future unfolds for our family, especially for our four grown children. And that means I am responsible for the outcome. I can choose to be small and childish, acrimonious or angry, but then I must claim what ensues. Like I am doing this morning.

A conscious parting will require me, again and again, to resist the automatic, unconscious choice of blame and contempt. It will require me to keep knocking off the bricks that want to build a wall of self-protection around me.

I may have learned to do these things too late. But I have learned them nonetheless.

2.

I met Fred as Juliet is said to have met Romeo – out on the balcony checking the weather. We were 25; he was my new next-door neighbor. I only remember the early morning sun, refracted by the buildings that stretched across the Chicago skyline and being rendered speechless by the browned, bare chest and faded Levis to my right.

He began frequenting our door at dinnertime. My roommate and I started finding little chores to keep him around such as fixing the wall phone or untangling the blinds – nothing too complex since he was banker and not a contractor. A little group socializing, a few late-night sessions of me feigning interest in chess, and pretty soon we were first-dating. We stayed up through the night watching the city sleep and then awaken, talking about literature, life and also kissing.

I'm sure I thought I was fully formed at 28 when we married. But how could I know what I would experience or who I was to become over the next 30 years?

In the months leading up to our wedding day, I tried in this way and that to shake him loose out of fear and a lack of self-worth. He had doubts too but a sense of integrity, and perhaps also some fear, tethered him to me. We did not talk about these things.

We cobbled together a rocky first year. When my birth family fell apart suddenly, I became unmoored, depressed and self-absorbed. He couldn't help. We didn't know how to talk about these things either. It was painful, so I packed it all away and moved on for the sake of our relationship.

I had probably been doing this with difficult emotions my whole life. I learned this from my parents as they most likely did from theirs.

3.

I was a serious little second-grader when a missionary nun visited my classroom at Immaculate Conception Grammar School. As she spoke, I was filled with a joyful recognition that I too was called to spiritual work. Not too much later, around the time when I had to confess my sins for the first time, I would learn how adept the church is at robbing the young and hopeful of their holy inspiration.

My teenage years and college days were punctuated unremarkably with equal amounts of spiritual awakening and self-destruction. Later, I stepped all the way off the spiritual path to devote myself to establishing a career and then a family. A decade passed in a blur of busy-ness. The more I ignored the undercurrent of subtle longing, the more I started to feel as unexceptional as an unflipped switch.

With my children off at school, I turned to art, and what I assumed would be a second career ended up being a period of intense self-reflection. I started to practice yoga seriously and found in it a promise of the peace I was seeking. When I delved deeper, I discovered that in order to get to the light, an opening to which we are all pulled, you have to walk straight and slowly through all your broken and scattered bits. I was born on that path; I could no less step off it than step in front of a speeding bus, though at times I could see the bus heading my way.

Outwardly, I was just as obsessively productive as I had ever been, but the inner work, on some days, absolutely overwhelmed me. I was unable to articulate or even understand what I was going through, and that allowed a distance to settle between Fred and me.

There was no overt dysfunction as there had been in my own family. We hardly disagreed much less argue and fight. No deceit, no belittling, no slammed doors. No observable signs of the impending danger, which was precisely why it was so dangerous. The damage was being done on the level of the unseen and unsaid.

If I could have then, I would have said: "I am here to witness the grace of life set against the backdrop of darkness. I am reconciling every notion that I am not Divinity itself by exploring every facet of disconnectedness. I am here to love myself back from separation to wholeness. This is a sacred mission that requires conquering every fear, forgiving myself for every unforgiveable thing I've ever done and facing the fact that I feel lost, unloved, unlovable, unworthy and worthless. I cannot stop until all the lies are untold and the route becomes clear: Self-Knowledge>Self-Acceptance>Self-Love>Sovereignty.

Who's with me?"

But I couldn't say those things because I was afraid to be seen as evangelical, crazy, uncool and unintellectual. And I very much wanted to be seen as the opposite of all that.

4.

As a young mother, I learned to bend my life around everyone else's. If I was good to myself at all, it could have appeared to others that I did what I wanted – a night out with friends, a yoga class or a spa visit. But, I did these things only after making sure everyone else's needs were met, after seeing that all were settled, after waiting to see what energy remained. Even the pets took precedence.

I planned and organized my family's lives and directed the nature of their relationships. It was a deeply satisfying role, but it left me feeling spent and resentful, not for what I had done, but for what I was not able to do. What was possible for me had to fit into the spaces not occupied by others. I became what I could with what was left over. I sacrificed my sacred potential. This is not what my loving family would have chosen for me. I gave them no choice. I did it out of a lack of self-worth and a need to control (which is really just fear).

I cried myself to sleep wondering how I could carry on feeling the way I did: angry, afraid, small, unseen, misunderstood, marginalized, defeated, unloved. I brought these with me into my marriage; the relationship made them impossible to ignore.

5.

Marriage, divorce, life – they are all mirrors showing me all the places in me that need healing. My places have signs indicating:

I am alone.

I am selfish.

I am not a good mother.

I am not a good person.

I am not capable of greatness.

I am not cut out for an exceptional life.

I am not deserving of joy.

I will not ever get this shit figured out.

I am unloved.

I am unlovable.

I am unworthy.

6.

I can't think of anything now except getting divorced and being divorced. I am questioning all my ideas about marriage.

I am wondering, if we hadn't relinquished our power to be in a relationship with one another to the state and the church, would we be in such pain now?

We alone defined who we were to one another before we stood at an altar and were married by a nameless priest we didn't know. A month before that, we had given our power to a faceless state when we secured the required license from a clerk who couldn't care less about us.

And so, because we had given them that authority once, here we are now returning to their poorly lit offices, seeking their approval, petitioning for their permission to dissolve our marriage.

What if instead we had kept the power of our relationship between us two? What if we had demonstrated to our children that a relationship is a living, breathing thing that changes every day and evolves over time and that we are the only ones responsible for how, and in what way, we honor this relationship?

What if we alone had chosen how to define our relationship: acquaintances, friends, passionate partners, shared parents, companions, domestic mates, co-grandparents or no descriptors at all? What if we had not sought outside permission but instead had let our own needs and desires dictate the terms of our relationship?

What if we had had no need for the word "divorce", an utterance that has triggered a cascade of emotional tumult for us all? Because in truth, we are what we say we are. We say we are family, and no one else gets to weigh in.

7.

If anyone were to ask me about my partner's flaws and shortcomings, I could produce a list. That seems easier than looking at my own list. But accusations don't get me where I want to go. I want to go where there is love, so I make a promise to talk only about what I am responsible for and it is this:

I was not a good communicator.

I was unable to clearly, bravely and unapologetically state what I wanted and needed.

I often acted and spoke unconsciously.

I found it hard to admit when I was wrong.

I buried my feelings because I didn't know how to deal with them.

I was unable to share my true feelings and beliefs.

I was not an especially good steward of our money.

I didn't know how to constructively express anger, fear and disappointment.

I sometimes failed to honor that my partner is also on a sacred, heroic human journey.

I tended to take the easy route of silent fury when vulnerability would have served us better.

I was sometimes selfish and sometimes childish.

I pretended things were fine when they weren't.

I made decisions that were not in his best interest.

I made decisions that were not in my best interest.

I blamed him for things I was responsible for.

I didn't know who I was.

I may not have tried hard enough to figure out who he was.

I gave up.

8.

There are times when the weight of what we are doing isn't quite so heavy, when the support I call in arrives in the form of good friends and other things to think about.

But unavoidably, my husband has become a plaintiff against the woman he has loved, supported and grown accustomed to calling his ally for almost half of his lifetime.

We are, in many ways, among the very lucky. Our separation is as amicable as it can possibly be. Our strategy has been to avoid the costly antagonism at which lawyers excel by working out every detail of our arrangement between us and utilizing counsel merely to legalize the language.

But it has been far from easy. We are both feeling raw and vulnerable – clearly not a comfortable state. And we are both worried about what our lawyers will persuade us, and each other, to do.

To remain conscious here has required me to soothe my own tender state so that I can remain compassionate toward my one-time partner, the man I have loved, supported and thought of as my ally for all these years.

This is a choice I make in every moment of this wrenching process. This is how I honor the love that has seen me through difficulty and celebrated my triumphs in our three decades together. This is the gift I give my children. This is how I allow love to do its magic and heal us all.

9.

People may believe it is easier to let go than to hang on, hang in there. In truth, they are both hard.

10.

I was in my 20s when a ticking time bomb finally imploded and blew my birth family wide open. My mother vowed to sew us back together again, but she didn't have the pattern.

I want to tell my children what I have learned about healing broken hearts:

> Allow yourself to be so incredibly, uncomfortably vulnerable that you think you may die from it. If you can step one precious toe on this road, a radical path will appear under your feet and everything else will just sort itself out.

11.

To My Dear Children,

I know you are heartbroken.

I am sorry.

I love you.

I always will.

I hope that is enough.

12.

I take the lead in "telling the kids", otherwise known as "breaking the hearts of those you love most".

It is every bit as dreadful as I imagine it will be, and in many ways worse because there is:

Thinking about your loved ones' pain, and

Experiencing your loved ones' pain, and then there's

Knowing that you are the cause of it.

The final being a category of deep anguish reserved especially for divorcing parents.

What's next for me is just as difficult. I must remain open and quiet in the face of emotions so strong and painful that there is no blood to the heart, no air for the lungs, no strength in the bones. All is in collapse. There is anger, devastation, confusion and sorrow. But it is not my turn to wail, as I would like to.

I have hurt my children with my actions, and I cannot offer defenses against what they think of me in this moment. It is not permissible for me to steal their experience by explaining it away. I won't allow myself to fall back on my habit of trying to make it easier for me by trying to make it easier for them.

I stand still while the fires of rage and grief lick at my feet. I do this the best I can.

13.

Upon my heart, I draft a recitation for my beloveds:

With the arrival of each new child, I am recalibrated in some essential way. It is both natural and radical that I slip so willingly and wholly into a profoundly unfamiliar second skin. I can no longer think of myself as singular or separate.

I spend the waking moments in careful attunement to my wordless infants. In the middle of the night, I ponder our hopeful future. Every glance is a love letter full of promises.

I am also a child in some respects since I am learning this role for the first time, every time. We are growing up together. Because I know nothing, there are countless heartbreaking missteps along the way. I have the inexperience and enthusiasm of an amateur. It can go either way – great victory or devastating loss. I pray it will go one way but know it will go both ways.

How can we manage this unmanageable feat of raising children without trusting that in the end, the love will be enough? That within them somewhere is a cellular memory of how much I have loved them in each moment, even the ones that carry forth my errors?

We can try to protect ourselves from experiencing loss by pretending we don't love, but this doesn't work, of course, because not loving is not possible. We have to trust that the brave heart knows its own resilience, and this is why it marches fearlessly into such dangerous territory again and again.

14.

Today I'm trying hard not to adopt two dogs. The dogs, of course, are meant to fill the void of all I am losing. Clearly, one dog isn't going to cut it.

I resist and instead sit here, uncomfortable with all the pain, disappointment and anger swirling around me, and try to love my broken self through it all.

I work hard not to spin stories in my head like these:

I have no parents.

I have no siblings.

I have no husband.

I have no family.

I have no sanity.

I have no future.

And, please note, I have no dogs.

My mind has arranged for imaginary thieves to steal the peace. I concoct horrible stories about how my children hate me, think I'm selfish, blame me. (Those turn out to be true, albeit temporarily.) I hear the melancholy echo of my solitary footsteps down the long hallway of our family home.

Those stories are only the distractions. What's real is this:

I am feeling a sadness so intense my bones ache with it.

I am scared. Of being alone. Of making a mistake. Of ruining my family. Of hurting everyone. Of being poor. Of growing old. Of everything.

I feel selfish for putting my own desires over the clear desires of everyone else.

I am angry and disappointed that my husband couldn't do what I wanted him to do or be what I wanted him to be.

I am embarrassed that I failed in my mission to stay married forever.

I am ashamed that I did not deliver on my promise to give my children an imperishable family.

I must be crazy.

I miss my dog.

I am cracked open, shattered, vulnerable, weak, tired, angry, confused, penitent, reluctant, contemptible, pathetic, right and wrong.

The never-ending torrent of tears is giving me deep wrinkles under my eyes.

I am crestfallen.

I am heartsick.

I am heartbroken.

15.

My first instinct as a mother has been to rush in and fix whatever makes my children feel bad. My parents never rushed in. They didn't seem capable of it. I thought my way cured their way, but I can see now how neither way allows for the healthy development and flexing of coping muscles. And that's what challenge does; it provides the resistance against which one grows stronger. And anyway, it isn't my job to prevent my children from facing challenges. And furthermore, I can't prevent them from facing challenges, as if challenges should be avoided at all costs.

At least this is what I tell myself now as night settles around my large and empty home. Guilt is a big fat pillow hovering overhead. It doesn't have to close in before it starts choking off the breath.

That guilt, or rather the avoidance of it, was enough to keep me fighting to save a relationship that didn't seem to be working for either of us. But one question persisted: Would I ever encourage my children to sacrifice their own happiness so that everyone else remains comfortable?

I grew up thinking that self-sacrifice was a noble gesture. If only it were this easy. The noblest thing is to walk the path of self-discovery even when that defies everyone else's expectations for us.

16.

At 19, our independent, bright-eyed, self-possessed and wildly creative only daughter is, rightly so, mad as hell that we put a crack in the only foundation she's ever known. It is almost too much for me to bear. I tell her "I love her beyond" and this is meant to convey that it is a love that defies definition, comprehension or logic. Knowing that our decision, and not just this one, has caused her pain leaves me feeling swallowed up whole by a sea of sorrow.

I want so badly for her to understand that it has taken every ounce of my courage and strength to make this agonizing decision. I want nothing more than to get to the part where she admires me for the hard choices I made, the part where she once again calls me her teacher, her guide, her friend.

I have to accept that today is not that day. And it may never come. And still, I had to say yes to the persistent call of my relentless heart.

17.

Out of nowhere, I miss my mother. I cry tears of regret I know she would wipe away. I didn't understand anything she went through in her life, and perhaps this is as it should be. My children will not know me in that way either. We can't really know anyone that deeply unless we are open to their labyrinthine humanity. We don't need access to the details to know everyone suffers with self-doubt, often finds self-love elusive and the march of time frightening. If we can't find compassion for others, it's only because we haven't given it to ourselves.

Sometimes now when I am falling asleep, curled up in a loose ball, I place a comforting hand around my own shin and hold myself tenderly like I would a child. On nights when sleep is slow to settle in, I place my hands over my heart and sense the radiating warmth of my own touch. And in that touch, I swear I feel the loving hand of God.

18.

Fred stopped wearing his ring months ago.

Eventually, and despite how exposed it makes me feel, I stop wearing mine. This seems to be a point of no return, but it will be several more months before I can wear any rings at all, not wanting to draw a bit of attention to my hands.

In conversation, I still introduce Fred as my husband. I think, what am I supposed to say? "This is my Fred." How do I confer that I love the person standing with me more than a stranger on the street if I don't use this word "my"? Is he no longer mine?

I suppose I am letting go in stages.

I am facing the fact that now I must hire people to do husbandy things like take the Christmas tree off the top of the car and hoist it into the stand while I hover nearby saying, "this way" then "back that way". Or sort out which electrical cords are essential to life, and which ones are just hanging around, refusing to be discarded.

This makes me feel incapable and somewhat pathetic, and for a moment I wonder if it is harder to let go of married habits than it was to let go of the relationship itself? Being married has crept into every corner of my life, and it will take some time for it all to seep out. One day I may be completely unmarried, but today, big parts of me remain so.

Later, I get the TV to work when it didn't and manage to connect my phone to the sound system when it wouldn't, and I can admit to attaching more triumph to these successes than they may merit.

19.

I am sorting through my feelings this morning – I don't want to be, but I am. I want to be sipping my coffee, watching the light gather around me. I want to be experiencing a deep acceptance of all that is and a slow rise of excitement for the breaking day. But I am not.

During a recent family outing that hadn't gone as well as I'd hoped, I learned I had been taken off the extended family text-message group. I felt the sting of rejection, the soreness of exclusion.

I can easily arrange a diversion; there are rooms to be cleaned, errands to run, friends to call, work to do. But our emotions are like scratchy patches on the skin; they keep calling attention to themselves.

As I sit inside the swelling sadness that seems out of proportion to the circumstances, I become aware of something deeper. It is grief over the fact that, because of my decision to divorce, my children will now have a life with their father and his family of which I cannot be a part.

And more. For all these years, I have been a sort of sun around which my children orbit. I have been the engine driving my family, organizing their activities and helping them maintain relationships with our large extended family. In choosing a new life for myself, I have chosen a new life for them, one that allows them, requires them really, to have lives that don't include me. I am being drawn out of perceptions of myself in the role of wife/partner and mother/sun.

And then comes the fear: Who am I exactly? And what have I done?

20.

I wake with a hollowness in my chest, remembering all the precious moments – days, weeks and years – my family has spent at our house near Lake Michigan where I am now holed up with my closest friend. She and I have come, as we have many times before, to walk, talk and watch the woods turn amber, scarlet and burgundy.

I have been returning to this area in all seasons since I was a child. My father stayed here with his parents, who themselves first stayed as newlyweds. When I came here as a teen, with the shaky sense of independence that a new driver's license affords, it seemed faraway, risky. I brought Fred here before we were married and each year after until we could afford a place of our own. Now, our children come here with their friends, making their own memories.

Now I am seeing everything as though for the last time. And, I can't help rail against the cruelty of having memory but not prescience so that I can see clearly what I've lost with no hint of what I will gain. What higher purpose does this serve except to leave me in doubt, regret and fear?

I return home Sunday afternoon in time to cook an early dinner. I have invited my daughter, Fred and a friend. I turn on a football game hoping the background noise will distract me from the loneliness climbing up into my throat. I call my son and then have to hang up when I start to fall apart. I am relieved when I hear Fred's car in the drive only to burst into tears when he hugs me. He is in tears too, but I don't know what they mean. I don't understand anything.

I wish I had more certainty. Shouldn't I be more certain?

Without some kind of faith, how do we go on? Is the absence of faith hope? What's left in the absence of hope? Presence?

After the house re-empties, I lie in bed thinking about Fred and wonder if I have made him feel unwanted or unneeded. I send him a text about a problem with the TV. He jokes that he has his hat in hand and is headed out the door. I let the sadness and my questions well up until I fall asleep.

21.

My daughter doesn't think we worked hard enough to fix our problems, and she has me second-guessing myself. She suggests that perhaps we're giving up too soon, too easily, which makes me wonder whether I have lost sight of something crucial. Did I not also believe that I could weather any storm with sufficient mettle, patience and time? She questions whether my lack of absolute certainty is a sign that there may be enough to work with. I don't know the answer. She believes that it is right and necessary to make sacrifices of the self for the benefit of all, and isn't there a part of me that also believes this? I can't seem to sort it all out, and I fear that my confusion is giving her, and me, a false hope, which might lead to a too costly compromise.

It's true that our situation lacks the obvious, outward confirmations that some marriages are better off ended. Things are okay, calm, functioning. Isn't good enough, good enough? I ask this question both for her and myself.

I face an impossible dilemma. How do I help her understand what's happening without defending my very personal reasons for it and in the process diminish her father? How do I let her inside a situation she can't possibly understand because it is not her experience? How do I teach her to follow her heart's call knowing that by following mine, I may be breaking hers?

I opt for the truth as I know it today, and also acknowledge that this may not be so tomorrow because as I change, my truth changes. For today, I explain that a relationship has to grow to flourish, and that if something is not vital with life, it isn't alive.

I tell her that there is no greater service to the universe than to honor the sovereignty of the Self regardless of how others feel about it.

I show her that we honor one another with compassionate honesty even when it is inconvenient, uncomfortable and difficult.

I stake my claim that everything we encounter is intended to help us expand in consciousness and grow in love, so that nothing is ever really wrong. On the path of sacred life, we can't ever take a wrong turn.

I tell her that the fear of making a mistake is the very thing beckoning us to jump.

I tell her that "good enough" just isn't.

22.

I feel compelled to travel, and so now, the Islamic call to prayer is wafting through my window, transporting me beyond time and place. It is beautiful and calming for reasons I do not understand, and I am at ease in the moment knowing there are millions of other souls around this mystical planet whose attention is being drawn to something outside of their small daily, sometimes frenetic, lives. The call to prayer is a call to presence – a constant asking to observe the sacred in our everyday lives.

I bring to mind the days, just after Fred and I had decided to end our marriage, when I became overwhelmed with a dark and irrational fear. I remember the feeling of devastation and my inability to get a grip, pull myself together or look on the bright side. I let myself again be pulled to that place where there is no peace, no hope and no joy.

The call echoes anew, reminding me that life is grace. Every part of it. I give myself the advice I would give my children:

Feel, Love, Heal.

Feel, Love, Heal.

Feel, Love, Heal.

23.

What more can we do than show up each day and try to learn what life has to teach us, even when it seems bent on teaching us that it is best to lay on the couch and watch TV?

24.

I see an image in my mind's eye of a woman running on the surface of a river that is flowing in the opposite direction. I can feel the effort it takes to keep from sinking, and I want to say, sister, just let go. Let yourself fall into the places you don't want to go. Let the river carry you downstream. It has carved an ancient route, and it wants you to get there effortlessly. There will be rapids, but you will not drown. Or perhaps you will drown but then bob to the surface when the river shallows.

I feel myself nearing the river's lazy bend, and I want to say, beloved sister, slow down. It is time to let go.

Part Two

You love me, and I find you still

A spirit beautiful and bright,

Yet I am I, who long to be

Lost as a light is lost in light.

Sara Teasdale, "I Am Not Yours"

25.

I am aware that I have strung together more good days than bad.

26.

I have just returned from a weekend trip to attend a wedding on the arm of my soon-to-be ex-husband. Neither of us wore our rings, but there was no confusion about our togetherness. We have done this so many times before – dressed up and presented ourselves as an "us". But I am struck by a sense of nostalgia and grief for lost things.

Sitting at our table watching the happy couple embark on their new life together, I find myself clinging to the small aspects of our relationship that are harder to let go of. Whispered conversation in a room full of strangers. Dancing after the sun has set. Leaning in for a photo. Laughing at his jokes, seeing how happy this makes him.

It's not like I haven't appreciated these small and meaningful things before. I have. It isn't like I don't see that a string of small moments creates a life. I do. What I don't know is why this isn't enough to sustain us. Why neither of us can settle for this as millions of people do.

At 57, with my children now on their own, I have never really lived alone and for some reason, I want to so badly. I long for the freedom to do as I please without informing or asking permission. Spend my time as I choose, walking as heavily as I want in my own footsteps. I want to build my own home, walk my own dog, exist in quiet spaces I have created.

In truth, I want to be alone, and I want to be together. I want my freedom without forfeiting the comfort and joy of the occasional small moments. It is selfish and probably unachievable, but mostly, it isn't what Fred wants. I offered him half a wife, half a marriage, and he drew the heartbreaking conclusion that he wanted and deserved more for himself. Whose fault is it that we both want what we want and need what we need? Who's to blame when the scale tips in a certain direction?

On the long drive back into the city, we talk about this place in which we find ourselves – an indeterminate pause between what was and what will be. Here, we are placing an improbably big bet that it will be better for both of us. Without that, how could we possibly tolerate the pain and uncertainty of where we are now?

On the bumpy flight home, I reach for his hand, and he holds mine right back.

27.

My daughter and I sit watching old episodes of *Dr. Phil* when the doorbell rings. It is somewhat late and we aren't expecting anyone, so I know immediately who it is since there is only one person who is allowed to ring doorbells around here at any time of the day or night. It's Jon.

Over the years, our neighbor Jon has shoveled snow from our walk, taken in trash cans, checked on us during storms, cleared tree limbs from our yard, sat with us on porches, lovingly chided our children, barbecued with us, jumped our cars, moved our furniture, replaced faulty water heaters, inquired about our parents, attended our events, counseled us on all things and been unfailingly present in our lives even when, and perhaps especially when, we might be tempted to lock ourselves behind closed doors. He's kept us laughing and crying and scratching our heads. Despite a family and challenges of his own, in a world of constant upheaval, he is as constant as one can be.

Appearing on our doorstep, familiar cigar in hand, he chokes back tears, offering us help now that Fred's absence has become permanent. He tells us he is here for us.

Every day there is a new sorrow. This one is for all the ways in which our decision is impacting him and others in our close-knit circle.

Our children have all grown up, our marriages are strained by circumstance and time, our parents are dying, our careers are concluding, our friends are struggling. This journey, the one that constantly threatens to defeat us, shows us how love ties us together forever and is the only thing we are never asked to relinquish.

28.

My small, fractured birth family never provided much support for me so, from the beginning, Fred's large family held a special appeal. There wasn't an easy or automatic acceptance, but I worked hard to cultivate the closeness I wanted and needed. Slowly, his people became my people.

When I began to suspect that my marriage might one day end, the fear of losing the family I had come to love kept me up nights crying into my pillow while my husband slept soundly beside me. But fear of loss is a shaky base for a relationship and ours continued to falter.

A month or so before our announcement, I stood in the driveway of my sister-in-law's home while her uncle described how he had helped his daughter and a couple of nieces "destroy" their spouses in divorce proceedings. My heart sank with the knowledge that I was about to join the ranks of the destroyed.

As news of our split spread, I was on high alert, watching for signs of who would be friend and who would be foe, judging each and every one, categorizing the rapidity and tenor of their response. I was like a newborn wild animal, separated from its mother, in a fearful frenzy of uncertain self-protection. It was devastating to be disconnected so suddenly from my pack, with whom I had raised children, celebrated countless milestones and shared a lifetime of experiences.

But because Fred and I had both worked so hard to lay the groundwork for a loving separation, he did not feel so threatened that he needed to close ranks against me. He encouraged his family to move beyond unexamined reactions and expectations to do what their hearts were calling them to do. And because of this, I was able to let down my defenses enough to allow that everyone is entitled to his or her own experience of this event.

We all walk around with invisible injuries that cause us to act in protective or aggressive ways when emotional danger looms. What else can we do in the face of such unbearable vulnerability? I only know that when I manage to touch my own invisible wounds with the hand of love, my heart softens to the experience of everyone around me.

29.

My father-in-law is dying; there's no denying it now. Divorce or not, I rush to his bedside to say goodbye and to support my mother-in-law, Fred's stepmother, with whom I am very close. I have not seen any of my family since they learned of our split. While I am worried about the new awkwardness, I have to go. Announcements aren't enough to release me from love and long history.

For the brief time I am in my father-in-law's home, I retreat to my comfort zone – the kitchen – and make meal after meal. There, I know I can process the uneasiness and also turn the inexpressible into the tangible. As I have always done, I let them know how much I love them by feeding them. I don't know who taught me how to do this, and I wonder if it is the last time I will do it.

There is a feeling amongst those of us gathered that something immense is fracturing. We did not anticipate the double blow of death and divorce, and now we are all clumsily trying to navigate a new normal no one wanted. They can't stop loving me on a dime – I am thankful for that. But I know that when the time comes for Fred to introduce them to someone new, their loyalties will have to shift. But for now, none of us can quite believe in that, and I'm so grateful for this bit of denial.

30.

We lie across from each other on hotel double beds, the result of a "mix-up" at the front desk. Perhaps we accept what fate has made because we are no longer afraid of its deft hand.

I ask him to tell me, once and for all, he doesn't want to be married to me. He can't but says something more telling when I ask how he's feeling, living apart.

He says he is lonely but doesn't miss me, my moodiness.

I tell him that I miss him, but I am not lonely.

I wonder if he hears, as I do, the subtle but splintering difference in these two answers. I realize I don't need him to because I think perhaps this message wasn't meant for him. And I am grateful for the blessing that has arranged for me to hear it.

31.

Saying goodbye to my wonderful, complicated father-in-law and saying goodbye to my family in the midst of un-marrying is too much for me so I miss the visitation and spend the day in bed with a migraine.

I don't think I can take another thing, and then I remember what the priest said when my young cousin died. It was simple as most truths are: The measure of your sadness is also the measure of your love.

During a quiet moment, I talk again to Fred about the questions I suspect are keeping me from moving forward. Even in the bottomlessness of his grief, he is resolute. I am grateful for this since I often allow others' desires to sway, and sometimes divert, my own. This is a liability of mine, not theirs.

At one of several post-funeral gatherings, Fred approaches and puts his hands affectionately on my shoulders. He asks me how I'm doing and then tells me that it is brave of me to be here. I feel a shift, and now I understand what my daughter has, on several occasions, suggested – that my presence here is confusing. They can't really become who they are meant to be without me if I am still here. I am a rock in the river. I feel the need to apologize. But instead, I say my goodbyes and head home.

On the drive back home, as my daughter dozes beside me, I am at ease. I step aside and stop interrupting the flow of life.

32.

Draft One of our Legal Document, which in one sense outlines what we have meant to each other, sits on my desk, pages unturned. Fred presses me to push forward with it, even though he has just lost his father.

I thought it kinder to wait.

He thinks it kinder to proceed.

Huh.

I realize that I have been stuck in a sort of limbo where I cannot progress without a few critical pieces of information. I tell him I need to say a few things and ask a few questions. His response, "Uh oh", is almost funny it is so familiar. I think, we are already divorcing, how much worse can it get? I am reminded that for him, some conversations may be worse than breaking up. And this is one of the reasons we are breaking up.

I want him to understand that our divorce is not my rejection of him. I need to say this because a part of me feels bad for him, and this has frozen me in place. I don't have the constitution to hurt him.

I want to remind him (because surely, I have already told him) that after 28 years of growing up and stumbling my way into early adulthood and 29 years of tending to the needs of others, it is time for me to become the master of my own life, to live it, unapologetically, on my own terms. I don't want to report to anybody, care for anybody or, for some indeterminate length of time, be with anybody. It's this last little bit that proves problematic.

In truth, I was willing to stay married but live somewhat separately and also together in some combination. And this leads me to my question: Why was that not enough? And this one: Do you think you will love someone else as much or more than you love me? And: Do you desire to love someone else as much or more than you love me?

Why am I, on my own terms, not enough for you? Is it the terms? Or me?

Or does he suspect, as do I, that my half-commitment is a half-fear of being fully on my own? Is my plan just a stepping stone that tricks me into believing I can't make it to the far bank in one jump?

And I have questions for myself too: Why was I not able to live my life on my own terms within the relationship? Is this even possible? It didn't seem so for me, but I am willing to admit, and not for the first time, that there's pretty much nothing that I know for sure.

33.

We don't like to be without a plan. A plan theoretically fills up a future space that we don't like to think of as empty. We really don't like empty.

A few months back, when I was anticipating that there would be a large empty space in my future, I thought about what I would do with that void, and that is exactly how I thought of it – a big nothing I would have to fill with something. And suddenly, out of nowhere came programs to enroll in, projects to take on, trips to make – chunks of something I could drop into my nothing. I considered all the options, but the nothing seemed so much more compelling.

Some time ago, a mentor encouraged me to ask my higher self what I should do to step into my full potential. The answer that came – stop teaching yoga – was both illogical and shocking. I remember thinking: What would I be if I was not a yoga teacher? Of course I knew that this was exactly what I was being asked to consider.

Really, I am being asked to stop dwelling in the smallness of what I'm doing and start playing in the bigness of what I already am.

I've slowly been stripped of almost every title I've taken on. Through death, I am no longer a daughter. Through time, not the mother I once was required to be. Through divorce, not a wife. Through choice, not a teacher. Even the roles I am playing as pet owner, homeowner, business owner, friend seem to have a very loose hold on me now. But instead of feeling that my life has become smaller and less meaningful, it seems more essential and full of pure potential. Instead of feeling lost, I feel found.

The universe doesn't always give us the explanations we would like. It dares us to trust in the illogical and shocking. We are asked to jump into the lake, knowing the bottom is very far from reach, and to believe that we will be held by the water.

34.

I receive news that an outrageous increase in rent may force me to move my yoga studio or shut it down and that I have just a few months to figure it all out.

The business has been a labor of love since its inception six years ago. It has given my life purpose, created a community I deeply desired, allowed for the fruition of ideas and been the catalyst for the friendships that sustain me today. Our lovely space has become a spiritual home for me and many others. I should be devastated. Particularly in light of all I've been through. But I am not. And this is more interesting to me than the news itself.

I have developed an unshakeable faith that there is a force orchestrating the best outcome for my greatest growth, happiness and freedom, laying down beads on the trail for me to pick up so that I don't get lost. I am past the naiveté that believes this path will be easy just because it is right. Often, easy is merely another name for safe.

I understand the appeal and contentment of safe, but safe isn't why we came here. I can see how I have been building my risk-reward tolerance. A mental image stays with me always: that I cannot grab onto the next rope until I let go of the one I'm holding.

I dream that I have entered a house while the owners are away. The two cats and a few family members I've brought with me are making a horrible mess of the place. I am desperately trying to clean it up before the owners arrive back home, but without much luck. There is another house around the corner that I have purchased and am trying to renovate. It is filled with inexplicable debris. All around me there are people pointing out problems, offering advice. But no one seems able to help me accomplish anything. I spend what seems to be a lifetime in this swirl of fruitless activity and halting progress.

In the morning, I can't shake the questions: Why am I spending my time and energy in houses that are not mine? What would happen if I just walked out the front door and away from it all?

I don't need to know what lies ahead. I just need to pick up the next bead laid at my feet.

Part Three

And how else can it be?

The deeper that your sorrow carves into your being,
the more joy you can contain.

Khalil Gibran, *The Prophet*

35.

Some days, the answers do not come. Some days, the questions themselves dissolve like salt in water. At first, the water is a bit murky, a little cloudy. You can stir it if you choose and this might hasten the process a bit. Or you can let it sit and arrive at the same place. Clarity.

Something has changed. I don't know yet whether it is tremulous or seismic, but I can feel its rumble.

This gives me a buoyancy made of equal parts relief and unexpected joy, maybe a pinch of guilt. And then something happens. My daughter, who has been appearing all day to be quite fine, who has been saying for weeks that she is fine, falls apart. Turns out, she is not fine. She is angry. She is a bottomless ocean of sadness filling with a fresh flood of salty tears. I note a new wisdom, but also the old hopelessness.

Mostly I listen, but sometimes I try out new ways of explaining things, and I am reminded what she has taught me best – people just want to have their hard, messy, unevaluated, unjustified feelings.

I notice that, uncharacteristically, my heart isn't sinking with hers. It is calm, still buoyant in the midst of my compassion for her. Is it possible that once the salt has dissolved and the water is clear, it can't go back to cloudy?

My daughter has spent the night. And in the morning, I hear her singing as she readies for the day.

36.

I have been beating the sun to the morning, sitting in darkness and observing the waking world. The cricket song has lost its urgency. I hear a mellow ebbing now that was not evident even a week ago, and I realize that every summer must enter its fall. It can be witnessed as a dying, but here in the Midwest, the beauty and splendor of autumn won't allow for much grieving.

Here in my home, there is a sense of the inevitability of the death of what we once knew. It almost comes as a relief after the unsettling protestations of an earlier season.

Because there is death. And what we have experienced is the demise of what we thought love should look like. As we gain the courage to let go of our grip on that version of family, we will see what love really is. We will watch as it unleashes its alchemy of healing, resuscitation and rebirth. It does this without our permission. Because this is what love does. It soaks us with divine magic even when we are most resistant. It changes winter to spring, darkness to light and us into ourselves.

37.

In the past twelve months, I've:

raced to my daughter's side in a moment of crisis,

witnessed my mother finally let go after 20 years of debilitating dementia,

put down my beloved dog,

worked deeply and painfully into my marriage,

started divorce proceedings,

broken my family's hearts and betrayed their dreams,

moved the last two of my four children out of our home,

lost friends and possibly a family,

said a final goodbye to my much-loved father-in-law,

felt scared to death and broken-hearted.

I have also:

been cared for and supported by the children I've raised,

watched them step up to comfort each other,

had my hand held by countless friends,

learned that the gift of grief is an admission of love,

forgiven and been forgiven,

decided that I matter,

come to believe that my presence has purpose,

known more love than I have ever known before.

It is a brisk and sunny day, and I am thinking about going for a walk. This has a certain poetry I can't quite decipher. No matter how dark life seems, there is a light asking us to walk on, if not closer. We don't know where the destination lies, or the best route, or even why we're going. But we understand the meaning of surrender – to know nothing and to trust completely.

Since we are asked to never and always let go, I lean, and sometimes fall, into the Allness of it all.

38.

I pick up my daughter at the train station, and afterward we buy a cartful of Halloween candy, contemplating how to come as close to just enough as possible.

She drags the decorations out of storage and scatters plastic bones in the yard while I pretend to scan a magazine. In truth, I can't take my attention away from how lovely and familiar it all feels.

The patter of excited young feet on the porch, the clang of our seldom rung doorbell, the uncontained cheers of "full size" take me back to my children's youth and my own.

Ritual reminds us we are in this together. An ordinary day becomes a gift set against a backdrop of intensity and change.

39.

The summer seemed to pass with an unbearable thickness, and now we are rapidly approaching the holiday season – our first in this new context. Our family unit has cracked open a bit, but the pieces haven't been flung too far from center. Our grown children have yet to marry, and technically we are still married, though that will soon change.

Biology and fate and perhaps something larger has brought us together, asking of us love, patience, tolerance, support, understanding and acceptance. We have imperfectly abided.

Though our children may resist it, we are individuals as well as parents, each with a precious life to tend and made ever more so for its waning. It is impossible for them, with so much life ahead, to see this from my perspective. Even now that my own parents are gone, it is difficult for me to recognize that their lives belonged to them, not me. Did I ever even see us as belonging to each other? I suspect I have always seen my life as mine and their lives only in relation to me.

For today, I release my need for my own children to see me in this light. I allow that it may not be in the nature of children to view their parents as individuals with lives to live. I vow to let them feel what they feel and be who they are. I accept that they may never see me as I do, but I won't let that stop me from tending this precious life of mine.

40.

Thank you page.

    Thank you keyboard.

    Thank you fingers.

    Thank you mind.

    Thank you heart.

    Thank you time.

    Thank you space.

    Thank you daybreak.

    Thank you darkness.

41.

I am keeping a secret from almost everyone. I am happy.

I don't know how to convince anyone that vast swathes of quiet with very little on the agenda make me feel more joyfully alive than anything I might be doing.

I can't explain how or why being alone sparks in me an inextinguishable hope for humanity. Or why being more myself connects me so inextricably to everyone else. Or how sorrow and grief and pain have filled my heart with so much love.

42.

A high wind sweeps through, scattering the days of November like leaves from the trees. It is almost Thanksgiving.

I am trying to remember the date we decided, once and for all, to end our marriage and can't quite believe it was only months ago. I have processed eons of grief since then, but I can't recall it and summon the same emotional intensity. I am beginning to believe that when they are fully experienced, the emotions leave no trace and they can't be triggered later, confounding us with an inexplicable potency.

Fred feels pressed to get out and engage in the world even though it seems more appropriate to stay in and fall apart. The life-death-rebirth cycle is inviting him into its loving embrace, but like most of us, he thinks that every sort of death should be resisted. As if we could hold back the very force of the universe.

We are asked to trust, and to believe that we are being held, guided, loved beyond our human understanding. That we will be okay.

We have to relinquish the control we think we have so we can begin to truly know how powerful we are.

From the floor above, I hear the shower turn on and am brought back to the years when my children rose before dawn to ready themselves for school. It is a comforting reminder, at the start of the day, that all is in order.

43.

I am seeing my family off for their first holiday without me. When I hug my husband, I notice a new thinness – one borne perhaps of stress and sadness in addition to age. I wonder if he feels less or more visible than when he was younger.

I have been the architect of my own invisibility, a job I inherited from my father who had a knack for making people feel unworthy. No matter what I did, I couldn't get him to see Me. And, oh, how I tried.

From my mother, I learned to be the author of my own diminishment. I learned how to be inconspicuous, how to wedge myself underneath someone else's light. I learned how to keep things peaceful by not making demands for myself.

My perfectly imperfect parents taught me how to love myself better by showing me where my gaps were just as I am showing my children where theirs are. Mother, father, husband, wife, son, daughter, friend, foe. There isn't anyone who doesn't show us how to love ourselves more and better. And so, no matter how difficult the circumstances, there is always something for which to be grateful.

It occurs to me that I am not only divorcing a husband but also the baggage I brought into our relationship. He is my teacher, not my enemy. From the depth of my soul, I am sorry. And from the bottom of my heart, I thank you.

44.

The past seems to have stretched out at a languid and measured pace, but now, it seems, we have been dropped into a supercollider where I await the inevitable collision. I know I will survive, but I will be changed in both nature and form.

I am grateful for the friends and family who have facilitated my growth and supported me so lovingly along the way. There is no doubt that each of us faces enormous life challenges, and it feels so sweet to help each other along.

Some days, I am sure that our souls have come to Earth to guide humanity back to the light after its long exploration of darkness. Other days, I'm convinced that our souls seek a shadow experience like a child seeks a flashlight at night. Either way, when I consider my fellow man, I see not the ways in which we play in the shadows, because God knows we do, but the essential courage, beauty and brightness of our essence. This is an endlessly discomforting place to be, but there is something undeniably vital happening here. I'm not exactly certain what it is, but I can feel the force that urges us on, championing our unknown cause. I do know that dark can't be seen inside of darkness, nor can light, cast against light.

45.

All day I have been wondering why my friends haven't reached out to ask if I'm going to the party or to try to persuade me.

Can't they imagine how hard it might be for me to attend a party by myself for the first time? Is it possible they don't care if I'm there? Or have they just forgotten me?

These self-pitying questions make no sense in light of the fact that I have no desire to go to the party. I have to remind myself that my complicated human feelings don't have to be rational.

A few weeks later, I am already in my pajamas when I see through the windows that my neighbors are greeting guests to their annual holiday party, a party to which we were invited last year and the year before, but not this year. Although I would so much rather be over here doing this than over there doing that, I register a pang of sourceless melancholy, and I dim the lights to keep from being seen.

46.

We have been given a court date of December 19 and now it's easy to become nostalgic or even romantic about all the other December 19s we've shared. I indulge for a moment and then realize it would be just as easy to recall the years that weren't so wonderful, the ones where there was more absence than presence, those in which the essential problem could be defined more by what didn't happen than by what did.

The past has a faded complexity, a nuance that can get worn down over time until it's a flat surface that looks one way from this angle and another way from that angle. The past lives somewhere nearby, and always will, but it does not live with us. It has already moved out, leaving a mere vapor trail, holding none of its substance or shape.

Why is it so hard for us to let go of something that's made of mist and fog?

On an errand in my little hometown, I run into an old friend who I don't see much anymore. She tells me she is sad to hear about Fred and me. Even though I knew a moment like this would come, I still stumble around, tossing out a few inadequate and oversimplified explanations, trying inexpertly to match the depth of my answer to the level of our intimacy. What else can be done – there on the street – the two of us not exactly confidantes? She asks me, "Can't you just work it out?" And I think, this is how incredibly stubborn the status quo can be. Even when it would have no real bearing on our lives, we resist change with all we have.

Life is a houseless home where there are no walls, no furniture, no fixtures. We have dreamed them up to give our lives solidity where none exists. And like it or not, we have an ever-present roommate who goes by the name of Nothing Ever Stays The Same.

47.

Christmas has long filled me with a clashing jumble of expectation, obligation, disappointment and devotion. This year that has been supplanted with the sweet peace of mind I must have been seeking always. Oddly, almost nothing is different except that I have let go of all but the love, and that has changed absolutely everything.

48.

And then I am notified that a particular social media outlet doesn't believe you can be in a relationship with someone who is not in a relationship with you. Very profound, Facebook.

The layers of painful disengagement seem endless. First there was the fraying. Then came the rapid and terrifying unraveling. And now, I guess, we are just chucking it all onto the Goodwill pile.

Have you ever gotten to Goodwill, only to become overwhelmed by sentimentality and start thinking that perhaps you shouldn't be getting rid of this thing or that?

Can you tell me, when you got back home, did you feel your space refreshingly tidied and more comfortable? Or did there seem to be something missing for a very long time?

Behind me, my grown children are playing a board game and in front of me, the holiday fire still burns. But soon they will be gone again, and the embers will have cooled, and I will still be here.

49.

As the calendar turns its final page of the year, I feel a sense of urgency. I dash off a note to my attorney, demanding that there be no more unnecessary delays. It seems imperative that I spend as much of the New Year as unfettered as possible.

I notice that people outside of my inner circle assume that Fred is leaving me. Even when I tell them we are both in agreement, I can see that they don't believe me, or worse, feel sorry for me. I am alternately fine with and mildly annoyed by this. Sometimes it feels like part of the greater patriarchy that is so subtle and so ingrained that we no longer even notice it. I'd like to get a divorce from that and perhaps I am.

With a little bit of distance, I can see the subtle ways in which I have placed myself in a deferential role. I might have believed it would be easier, but I didn't understand the cost. To his credit, my husband would occasionally see the imbalance of power and try to correct the course. I could have offered solutions or demanded more, but I didn't value myself enough. So, I sat in a gilded cage of my own making, ignoring the key gripped in my talons. Failure of the imagination is the saddest form of it.

I feel a great rising now, not just of myself but of us all. I hear evidence of it in the cultural vernacular – the languages of love and light being spoken everywhere I go. Because I speak sweetly to myself now, it makes it almost impossible to hear harshness anywhere.

50.

Happiness comes and goes. It's emotional, tangential. Joy is everlasting and underpins everything. It's a state of being made of peace and acceptance and contentment and clarity and reverence and generosity and kindness and love. Happiness is a note. Joy is music.

We think that places and people and thoughts and jobs and ideas will bring us joy when in reality it is the other way around – our joy points us to the right places, people, thoughts, jobs and ideas. And as we become more adept at allowing this grace in to our lives, we barely have to question whether something is right or wrong for us. We just know. And there's no judgment involved. We don't need reasons why a person or situation isn't right for us. It's just a grateful yes or a loving no.

When I hear that my husband has plans for New Year's Eve, I feel a wave of anger and sadness which turns toward suffering the longer I allow my imagination to run its play of possible scenarios.

As midnight approaches in my life, I sweep my attic floor, light some candles and arrange a few crystals. I tear little pieces of paper and on them write meaningful things that need to be acknowledged and released. And then I burn them over big steel bowl, watching the smoke rise and vanish. I welcome in the New Year and its promise of peace, acceptance, contentment, clarity, reverence, generosity, kindness and love. I allow my joy to bubble up like champagne.

51.

I am aware of the inherent Divinity in every single moment. It can appear as grief, frustration, anger and despair just as easily as it can appear as bliss, joy and connection. When I see each moment as a blessing bursting with depth and purpose, there is nothing that doesn't warrant my full and spacious gratitude. When I open to it, I anchor in an explosion of consciousness chock-full of richness, truth, beauty, wonder, awe and inspiration. It's there like a ripe plum growing from a low-hanging branch right in front of me. I barely need to lift a finger to pluck it off.

At times I have felt so small that the bigness of it all was frightening to me. And when I have tried to figure it all out with my mind, I couldn't. It doesn't make sense there. It must find the heart. As I let go and rest in the not knowing, I can feel the magic entering, and I am no longer afraid despite my position here on this precipice. I am tempted to wander in or test a toe but know that it is my destiny to be bold and brave and jump so that I can be carried like a glittery particle on a sudden breeze, sweetly stunned by the mystery of it all. Like something that is seen only in the glint of the sun.

52.

Week by week our relationship continues to shift and now we see each other less than we talk on the phone. It used to be the other way around.

I hear a playfulness in Fred's voice that has been missing for a very long time, and I am filled with happiness and hope for him.

I notice a softening in our conversation, and I feel uncommonly content to linger in it, not suppressing an urge to rush off.

He expresses genuine concern for me, and I listen to him without judgment, and I begin to appreciate that this is what I have always longed for, from both of us.

Is it possible that slowly, somewhere along this journey, we are learning, perhaps for the first time, how to really love each other?

53.

I consider my two options: I can review this pile of official paperwork for the tenth time. Or I can text my husband to tell him that I am thinking of him with love.

I choose the latter.

54.

I don't know if it's true what my astrologer friend says that Fred and I are resolving thousands of lives together, but it does feel like we are doing the real, deep work of this lifetime.

I've sat on the divorce documents for weeks and now Fred is aggravated with my lawyer and his. When I suggest he should be annoyed with me since it was my fault, he says he doesn't want to be, and this means so much more than if he had just dismissed the idea or denied it. And I feel the same way. What's the point now of holding on to frustration, anger or disappointment? I wonder if there ever was.

The healing process has required me to examine every emotion, following the thread back to its origin, and I have learned that the real cause is rarely what I thought it was. Sometimes I find a wound so old I can't even carbon-date it. I know now I have unconsciously avoided the emotions that surround these ancient scars because I think it is the safer thing to do. But unfelt emotions never heal; they only fester. Felt emotions, turns out, are like salt to the wound –stinging just briefly before forever healing.

I have learned that self-love is the antidote to everything, and there isn't anything that it cannot tame or thaw.

55.

My tendency is to explore every aspect of every scenario, mining it for details that might shed light on my journey or perhaps illuminate the road ahead, and this is how I stumble upon the notion that it might be possible that my husband wanted to leave me much earlier than he would be willing to admit. I have no idea if this is really true or not, and maybe I don't need to know, and I might never know anyway because Fred's tendency is to keep the details unruffled, focusing instead on acceptance and moving forward because what does it matter who did what, when and why. We are here now.

There is perfection in his approach because it is his. There is perfection in my approach because it is mine. They are both right and true and rich with potential to spur our evolution together and apart.

We can get so tangled up in each other's process, trying to figure out why they do what they do instead of understanding what motivates our own thoughts and actions. Perhaps we do this because it's easier and less painful to blame than to take responsibility. It may seem safer to stay seeded underground than to face the wicked elements as a tender shoot. But of course, there's no flowering then.

The path is strewn with rocks and adversaries. When I reach out to hold my own sweet and uncertain hand, I grab hold of my family and the whole of humanity and, because compassion is the mightiest muscle, my load grows lighter with each step. Burdens are nothing more than reminders that I am lucky to bear and sometimes buckle under them.

56.

If we are being very honest, there is something mutual in all divorces.

Something in you both knows when the relationship no longer serves you, when it, or any situation really, is feeding your soul or whether it has begun, almost imperceptibly at first, to diminish the effervescent life force that lets you know you are fully alive.

You can bury it under many years and a thousand layers of justification like:

It's better than nothing.

The children will be devastated.

I am afraid.

I don't want to be alone.

We can't afford it.

I'll have to start over.

It's easier to stay.

I don't want to disappoint anyone.

It will be painful.

I made a promise.

Who will take care of me?

It's not that bad.

This is what I signed up for.

Maybe it will get better.

And while you are engaged in these negotiations with yourself, there already will have been some slight shift, also imperceptible at first, in your state of mind and then your behavior. Still, you can ignore the beckoning for many years and in a thousand ways such as:

work more,

see friends more,

shop more,

eat more,

gamble more,

pray more,

play more,

travel more,

exercise more,

do more,

ignore more.

But you can't unask a question. You can't unknow the answer once you do. And you can't stop your life from wanting to be fully alive.

57.

I am anticipating the day that will be the demarcation between married and divorced. There will be not just a day but an hour, a minute, a moment, an instant. Is there going to be a fucking gavel? I don't know, but the thought of that makes me miserable. It isn't something that I really want to experience. But I can't know in advance what that moment will really be like so why dwell in the unknowable future?

We meet to trade mail and documents, some words, but I am sick and don't feel strong enough to say the things I want to say. He takes out my trash, offers to make me tea. In this way, he is here for me today. Maybe he will be here for me tomorrow if I need him. I don't know this either. But in truth, we never do.

58.

I have a very bad terrible day when everything hits at once, and I immediately run through my checklist of people who might make me feel better. My husband is still at the top, but so are friends, family members, soul sisters and children. It could be worse I suppose – the list could include shopping, cigarettes, gin, chocolate, toast, porn, pills, etc. Not saying some of those haven't been on the list in the past, but they are not today. There is a difference, I think, between needing someone to hold your hand through it and dodging it altogether. I know this because no amount of phone calls, texts and visits could stem the flow of yesterday's tears.

59.

What sense does it make to vow:

I will feel for you until death just as I do now.

I will stay with you, in this way, forever and ever, no matter what.

No amount of time or circumstance will change who we are to one another.

This is what makes sense to me now:

In the name of love, I have encouraged you to dig a long and perilous tunnel from the most vulnerable parts of your heart to mine.

Perhaps I have persuaded you to forget about the tunnel and instead crash through the front gates.

True love is an incomparable, unfathomable act of courage, and you have attempted this daring crossing for me.

We may close up the tunnel, shut the gates, but I will never betray this, the bravest of acts.

Part Four

This is the miracle that happens every time to those
who really love:

The more they give, the more they possess.

Rainer Maria Rilke, *Letters*

60.

My husband has become my ex. I hate this semi-word but "former" sounds like someone has lost their job, which I suppose is true in a way. I decide to try on "one-time". It will take twice as much effort to say this, but I think it is worth it.

We get to choose how we experience everything but often opt for the societal norm without giving it much thought. It's easier to go along than to be perceived as bucking the trend, and this is how societal norms, even the bad ones, form and perpetuate.

Up until the final moment, my attorney tries to persuade me to draw the case out, dig deeper, get more. It is a societal norm that a divorce attorney's role is adversarial and that getting more money or property or leverage is better than fostering peace, cooperation, trust and love. It requires great vigilance on my part not to be swayed by her attempts, under the guise of protection, to erode the belief I have in my one-time partner and our ability to create a new norm – one that recognizes that fighting over scraps cannot make a banquet.

A lack of trust is just our own fear of not being treated fairly, which is a thinly disguised way of saying we don't feel safe, loved, lovable or worthy. What if, at this most vulnerable disclosure, we turn the love we desire to feel from others onto ourselves and discover that this is the only way not just to be healed but to be freed forever from the oppression of scarcity, the terror that there is not enough love for us.

It would be like finding that there's no bread at the grocery store only to realize there is an endless supply of flour, oil, water and salt, and you can bake your own damn loaf. And it tastes much better.

Relationships severed by divorce or death or some other parting are much more painful when we believe the love has ended. We are not fighting over the stuff, the money and the kids. We are struggling with the love we feel is lost to us and the hope that the stuff, money and kids will fill the gap.

When I think that I have lost my one great love, my family, our life together, I am overcome with sadness and grief. When I realize I haven't actually lost any of that but have it all still, but in a new form, I am consoled and fortified. I am just as abundantly blessed today as I was yesterday.

61.

There is a peace between us now. We get to be in each other's lives because and when we want to not because we have to. We're not filling roles we thought we had to. We are capable of far more than we think we are. We are more powerful than we imagine we are.

62.

I was born loving my children even before they were born or lost. I think I was born loving Fred too since I knew it the instant I first saw him, and I love him still. This is how I know love outlasts everything. This is how I know that love is everything.

63.

I make a very big decision without consulting anyone. Weeks later, I am still savoring the sweet foreignness of this and it makes me wonder if I have ever done it before.

Is it the freedom to make my own decision that feels so satisfying? Or the decision itself?

Or is it the exhilaration of fully trusting the absolute infallibility of my inner wisdom that has me swooning still?

I have never felt a rightness so right as this, and only I know the layers of worry, unworthiness, unconscious thinking, doubt, shame, guilt, pressure, expectation and conditioning I've had to dig through to get here.

It is a place of such unexpected joy.

64.

My mind clamors like anyone else's but I have learned how to let it head off without following it down that chaotic road. Instead, I find comfort in the quiet that occurs in the split second between what is and what will be that stretches out indefinitely. There, calamitous uncertainty is revealed as limitless potential so that "I don't know what's going to happen" is easily rephrased as "Anything can happen".

I have the sense of having walked through a doorway into an unanticipated freedom. It's not a freedom from relationships because I have those still, and they keep me gratefully bound. It feels more like stepping into my own skin where ease and difficulty, light and dark, and all the polarities are reconciled into one whole truth.

Throughout my life, I've tried on all kinds of costumes, constantly and sometimes frantically, throwing off one in favor of another. And often, I would have the sense of having chosen the wrong one, like showing up at the PTA meeting in my scuba gear.

The true Self is naked, not just un-costumed. To say that it takes a lot of guts to show up with nothing on is an understatement, and yet this is what we are asked to do, all day, every day.

Grocery store. Naked.

Coffee with friends. Naked.

Business meeting. Naked.

Family outing. Naked.

Birthday party. Naked.

Blind date. Naked.

Wedding day. Naked.

Difficult conversation. Naked.

First day on the job. Naked.

Last day on earth. Naked.

It is enormously difficult work we do each day, and everyone we meet is doing it, either consciously or unconsciously. The only thing that makes sense is to cultivate a brazen compassion, especially for ourselves.

I try to keep this in the back of my mind, and it allows me to see every situation in a softer light.

65.

I finally may have learned that being able to fully feel and then accurately describe how I am feeling is a skill as critical to the success of a relationship as truly hearing what my partner is saying about how he feels.

Seems obvious, easy. But it wasn't for me.

My marriage had pretty much collapsed from within before I gained the courage to understand and communicate what I was thinking and feeling. I could call to mind the reasons why Fred made this difficult for me over the years, but ultimately, I am responsible for my actions. I am the one who did not say what needed to be said. I am also responsible for my contribution to the atmosphere in which his attempts to communicate with me fell flat, were misunderstood, ignored, triggered me, threatened my ego, made me feel vulnerable and brought up my insecurities about being unworthy and unlovable.

In the end, I gained the courage to speak my truth as I knew it, with the understanding that I had no control over how it was received. Sometimes what I thought was true, was not. And rather than turn a blind eye to this discovery, dig in my heels, hang onto an erroneous version of my story, I had to admit that I was wrong.

I had to learn to listen in silence when every ounce of me wanted to lash out, defend myself, pick apart the argument, present my position, refute, complain, get righteous. As I was working to become more consciously aware of myself, I was able to recognize a certain way of being in my body when confronted with uncomfortable subjects. I would feel my muscles contract, my shoulders hike up, my tongue press to the top of my mouth. When I became aware of this, I reminded myself to breathe slowly and deeply. This physical softening would lead to a mental and emotional softening. This mindful internal work facilitates an opening to the idea that the one in front of us is human, doing the best they can in trying circumstances, wants to be heard and, if at all possible, understood. But mostly just heard.

Although we could not ultimately curve our paths back together again, better communication gave us the tools to peacefully negotiate our split and establish a positive relationship for the future.

66.

Dining alone tonight?

Yes. I am.

I have taken myself away on a writer's retreat, ironically, to a place that is crawling with couples, not intentionally of course, but I don't believe in accidents. I am supposed to be writing, but I can't help observe them instead. I want to categorize each pair but it's difficult, and, I recognize, unfair. Those two seem happy, but what about later when he makes a mess of the butter at dinner or she starts helping him with the driving. I can't hear what that couple is saying, but she is very emphatic about it while he just nods. Is he thinking about the lovemaking that will occur later or counting the minutes until she falls asleep in the chair?

I inadvertently make eye contact with one man strolling the beach, and he quickly drapes his arm around his wife, maybe for protection.

Some don't seem to have much to say to each other. Every marriage has its own language, so it's impossible for me to judge if this is good or bad.

I see another couple walking together and notice that their steps are almost comically syncopated. Is he shortening his stride for her or is she lengthening hers? Neither gait seems natural. I assume they are very practiced until they draw near and I see that they are very young. This makes more sense. Older couples almost never walk that way together. Sometimes they don't even walk side by side. Or hold hands or link elbows. Sometimes one walks well ahead of the other shouting back this or that. It could just as easily be the one from behind who does the shouting. Either way, they almost never hear what the other is saying, but that doesn't necessarily cause them to come closer to one another. Some couples look like they are in a dreamland of their own. Some appear to be in a matrimonial prison.

I don't have any recollection of seriously contemplating my future. I don't remember thinking about being married or seeing myself with children. I never wanted to grow old with someone or to grow old alone. But I suppose I assumed things. For a very long time, I assumed I would be with Fred. Even later, when I feared I might not be, a part of me still assumed I would be.

We have been apart for months now, and I miss him. I haven't gotten used to the idea that we are no longer married. I don't feel regret, but perhaps that is because, on some level, I am still making assumptions. Or maybe it's that after so much life together, so much adjusting our gait for the other, we haven't yet learned to walk independently of one another. Maybe the distance between our steps will just grow and grow until we lose sight of each other and can no longer hear what the other is saying.

It's just too soon to tell.

67.

At dawn, I feel the softness and ease of my breath just after waking. With each inhale, I push a bit further into the unknown. When I cling to what is known out of fear, I restrict the flow of life. I remember that I am the breath, and the Divine is breathing me. There can be no separation between breath and breathing. So, I loosen my grip and the air becomes soft again.

68.

I awake with a prayer. There is nothing outside of Divinity. We are held in its silvery web; we float in its grace. And if it has created its own dark corners, mine must be holy too. I feel myself surrendering into the effortlessness, comfort and power of knowing that I am never outside of its sacred plan. And this will always be so.

A decade and a half after college, an offhand comment by a one-time friend left me feeling flattered that he had thought so highly of me and simultaneously ashamed of my lack of accomplishment. Had he seen something in me that I had missed? Or had I seen it and squandered it? Throughout my life, I have believed that, despite my potential, I was repeatedly falling short. I despaired, never able to pinpoint what had gone wrong. I felt untapped, passed by.

But I have listened to the years and their wisdom. I now know that what I was missing was not the accumulation of accreditations, designations and assets but the understanding of the inherent grandeur of just Being. I can see myself as a daughter, wife, mother, lover, but titles are fleeting, not fixed, because we are verbs, not nouns. I am the act of curiosity. I am the expressing of love in the present tense. As God extends her hand, and the cosmos is expanded, I am the reaching.

I step into the shower, and when the glass door becomes steamy, I draw a big heart with my finger. And in its center, I write my own name.

Notes